MW01123161
DECEMBER 7, 1787
ILLINOIS
IOWA
KANSAS
MONTANA
STATE OF OREGON
1859
OKLAHOMA
WISCONSIN
1848

First published in Great Britain in 2002 by Brimax
An imprint of Octopus Publishing Group Ltd.
2-4 Heron Quays, London E14 4JP

A CIP catalogue record for this book is available from the British Library.

ISBN 1 85854 422 X

Created by ticktock Publishing Ltd.
with illustrations by Chris Hill

Printed in China

Children's USA

by Ronne Randall

Contents

The United States of America

The flag of the USA is known as "The Stars and Stripes". The thirteen stripes represent the thirteen colonies that became the very first states after the American Revolution (1775-1783). Today there are fifty states, with a star on the flag for each one. The country's national anthem is even called "The Star Spangled Banner"!

Scale: 621 miles
1000 km.

The US Capital

Washington, DC (District of Columbia), has been the US capital since 1800. The White House is the home of the US president, and Congress meets in the Capitol Building. About 572,000 people live in the city.

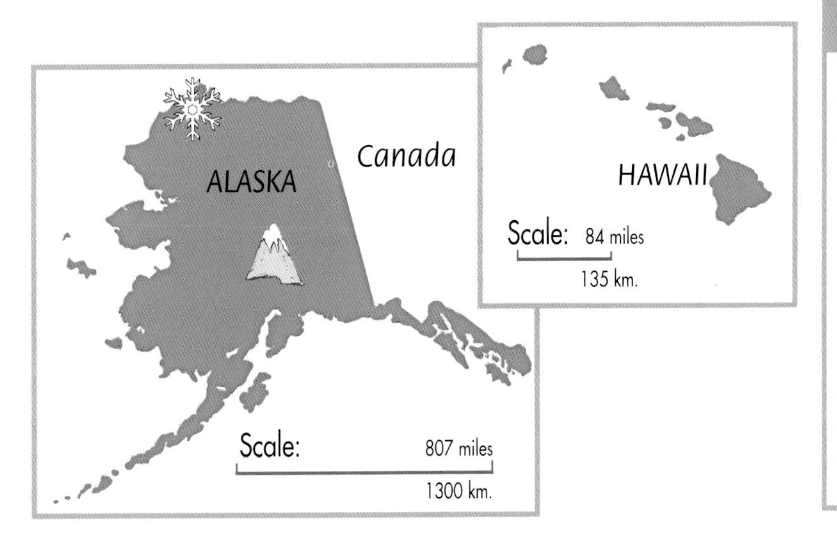

USA fact file

Highest mountain: Mt. McKinley, Alaska – 20,320 feet (6,194 m.)

Longest river: Mississippi – 2,350 miles (3,782 km.)

Largest city: New York – population 8,008,278

Deepest lake: Crater Lake, Oregon – 1,932 feet (589 m.)

Coldest place: Barrow, Alaska

Hottest place: Death Valley, California

Tallest building: Sears Tower, Chicago, Illinois – 1,450 feet (442 m.)

Total US population: 281,421,906

State fact file

Population

State flower

State bird

State tree

Look out for these pictures and check out the state facts throughout the book

Population figures supplied by US Census Bureau – Census April 2000

State fact file

Connecticut

3,405,565

Mountain laurel

American robin

White oak

Capital City: Hartford

Nickname: Constitution State; Nutmeg State

Maine

1,274,923

White pine cone and tassel

Chickadee

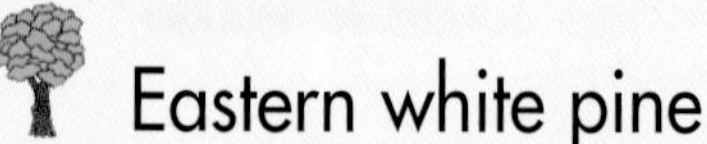

Eastern white pine

Capital City: Augusta

Nickname: Pine Tree State

Massachusetts

6,349,097

Mayflower

Chickadee

American elm

Capital City: Boston

Nickname: Bay State; Old Colony

New England

The coastline of this region was mapped in 1614 by the explorer Captain John Smith, who came from England. The land reminded him of home, so he named it New England.

Fall Leaves

Every fall, thousands of "leaf peepers" come to New England to see the breathtaking colors of the fall leaves. The colors are at their best between late September and mid-October.

The first place in the USA to see the sun each morning is the peak of Mount Katahdin, the highest spot in Maine.

Thanksgiving

In the fall of 1621, America's first Thanksgiving was celebrated in Plymouth, Massachusetts. The Pilgrim settlers invited their Native American neighbors to join them in a three-day feast and celebration.

Did you know?

The American Revolution began in Massachusetts, with the Battle of Lexington, in April 1775.

Blueberry Pie and Pancakes

Vermont is the USA's biggest producer of maple syrup, and Maine grows ninety-nine percent of the USA's blueberries – so, if you like blueberry pie and pancakes, New England is the place to be!

State fact file

New Hampshire

 1,235,786

 Purple lilac

Purple finch

 White birch

Capital City: Concord

Nickname: Granite State

Rhode Island

 1,048,319

 Violet

 Rhode Island red hen

 Red maple

Capital City: Providence

Nickname: Little Rhody; Ocean State

Vermont

 608,827

 Red clover

 Hermit thrush

  Sugar maple

Capital City: Montpelier

Nickname: Green Mountain State

State fact file

Delaware

783,600

Peach blossom

Blue hen chicken

American holly

Capital City: Dover

Nickname: Diamond State; First State

Maryland

 5,296,486

Black-eyed Susan

 Baltimore oriole

 White oak

Capital City: Annapolis

Nickname: Cockade State; Free State; Old Line State

New Jersey

 8,414,350

 Purple violet

 Eastern goldfinch

 Red oak

Capital City: Trenton

Nickname: Garden State

Northeastern States

The Northeast is considered the gateway to the USA. It also became the nation's birthplace on July 4, 1776, when the Declaration of Independence was signed in Philadelphia, Pennsylvania.

Statue of Liberty

Standing 305 feet (93 m.) high in New York Harbor, the Statue of Liberty welcomes people to the USA. She was a gift from France in 1886.

Amish Country

The Amish, who came from Germany in the 1700s, still lead simple, traditional lives with no modern conveniences, in Lancaster County, Pennsylvania.

Empire State Building

New York City's Empire State Building has 102 floors. There are 1860 steps from street level to the top, 6500 windows, 73 elevators and 70 miles (118 km.) of water pipes.

Waterfalls

Niagara Falls, between northwestern New York State and Ontario, Canada, is actually two waterfalls – the Canadian Horseshoe Falls, 161 feet (49 m.) high, and the American Falls, 167 feet (51 m.) high.

State fact file

New York

 18,976,457

 Rose

 Bluebird

 Sugar maple

Capital City: Albany

Nickname: Empire State

Pennsylvania

 12,281,054

 Mountain laurel

 Ruffed grouse

 Hemlock

Capital City: Harrisburg

Nickname: Keystone State; Quaker State

Maryland is the narrowest state in the USA. At Hancock, in western Maryland, it is only about one mile (1.6 km.) wide.

State fact file

Florida

 15,982,378

 Orange blossom

 Mockingbird

 Sabal palmetto palm

Capital City: Tallahassee

Nickname: Sunshine State

Georgia

 8,186,453

 Cherokee rose

 Brown thrasher

 Live oak

Capital City: Atlanta

Nickname: Peach State; Empire State of the South

North Carolina

 8,049,313

 Dogwood

 Cardinal

 Pine

Capital City: Raleigh

Nickname: Old North State; Tar Heel State

Southeastern States

This part of the USA is known for its warm, sunny weather, which attracts tourists all year round. Cotton, peanuts, and many fruits and vegetables are grown here.

American Alligators

The thick swamps of the Florida Everglades are home to many exotic plants and animals, including American alligators. They can grow up to 19 feet (5.8 m.) long

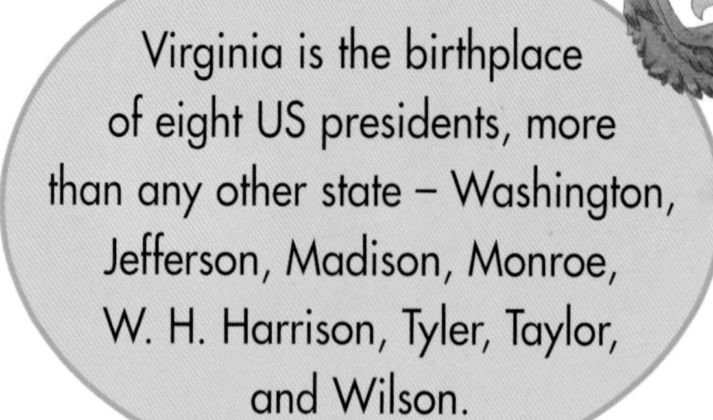

Men on the Moon

The *Apollo 11* spacecraft, which took men to the moon for the first time, was launched from the Kennedy Space Center in Cape Canaveral, Florida, in July 1969.

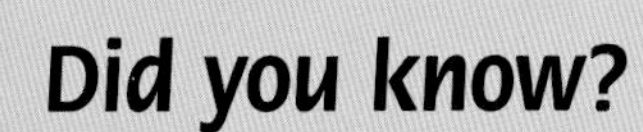

Did you know?

The first airplane flight in history, made by Wilbur and Orville Wright, took place at Kitty Hawk, North Carolina, in 1903.

Dr. Pemberton's Invention

Coca-Cola was invented in May 1886 in Atlanta, Georgia. Its inventor, a chemist named Dr. John S. Pemberton, originally sold it as a headache cure!

State fact file

South Carolina

4,012,012

Yellow jessamine

Carolina wren

Palmetto

Capital City: Columbia

Nickname: Palmetto State

Virginia

7,078,515

Dogwood

Cardinal

Dogwood

Capital City: Richmond

Nickname: Old Dominion

West Virginia

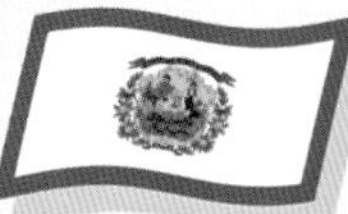

1,808,344

Big rhododendron

Cardinal

Sugar maple

Capital City: Charleston

Nickname: Mountain State

State fact file

Alabama

4,447,100

Camellia

 Yellowhammer

 Southern longleaf pine

Capital City: Montgomery

Nickname: Camellia State; Cotton State; Heart of Dixie

Arkansas

 2,673,400

 Apple blossom

 Mockingbird

 Pine

Capital City: Little Rock

Nickname: Land of Opportunity

Kentucky

 4,041,769

 Goldenrod

 Cardinal

 Tulip poplar

Capital City: Frankfort

Nickname: Bluegrass State

Southern States

At 2,350 miles (3,782 km.), the Mississippi is the USA's longest river, flowing from Lake Itasca, Minnesota, down to the Gulf of Mexico, through part of this region. Its famous riverboats have been sailing since 1811.

Mardi Gras

New Orleans, Louisiana, is known as the birthplace of jazz music. It is also famous for the colorful Mardi Gras carnival that takes place every February.

Did you know?

The world's first electric trolley system began running in Montgomery, Alabama, in 1886.

Thunder over Louisville

The Kentucky Derby is the oldest and most famous horse race in the USA. The race's opening festival ends with "Thunder over Louisville", the world's biggest fireworks display.

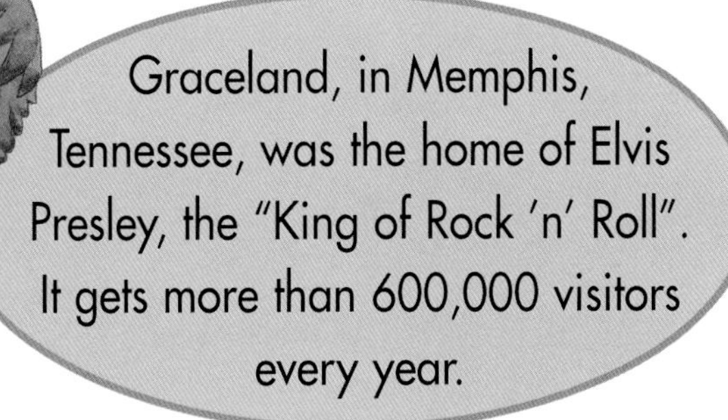

Graceland, in Memphis, Tennessee, was the home of Elvis Presley, the "King of Rock 'n' Roll". It gets more than 600,000 visitors every year.

Gold Bullion

Another famous Kentucky attraction is Fort Knox, near Louisville, where most of America's gold bullion is stored. It holds over six billion dollars worth of gold – more than anywhere else in the world!

State fact file

Louisiana

  4,468,976

 Magnolia

Eastern brown pelican

 Cypress

Capital City: Baton Rouge

Nickname: Pelican State

Mississippi

 2,844,658

 Magnolia

 Mockingbird

 Magnolia

Capital City: Jackson

Nickname: Bayou State; Magnolia State

Tennessee

 5,689,283

 Iris

 Mockingbird

 Tulip poplar

Capital City: Nashville

Nickname: Volunteer State

State fact file

New Mexico

1,819,046

 Yucca

Roadrunner

 Piñon

Capital City: Santa Fe

Nickname: Land of Enchantment

Oklahoma

 3,450,654

 Mistletoe

 Scissor-tailed flycatcher

 Redbud

Capital City: Oklahoma City

Nickname: Sooner State

Texas

 20,851,820

 Bluebonnet

 Mockingbird

 Pecan

Capital City: Austin

Nickname: Lone Star State

Southwestern States

Much of the Southwest's history and culture comes from the Native Americans who have lived there for centuries, and the Hispanic peoples who have settled there. The region is rich in natural resources, such as gas and oil.

Pueblo Native Americans

The Pueblo Native Americans of New Mexico have lived in the same area for more than 1,000 years, longer than any other people in the United States.

The narrow part of western Oklahoma is called the Panhandle, because it looks like the handle of a frying pan.

Cow Chip Throwing

Beaver, Oklahoma, is "The Cow Chip Throwing Capital of the World"! Every April, a World Championship Cow Chip Throw is held here. Of course, the cow chips are dried before they are thrown!

First Rodeo

The world's first rodeo was held in Pecos, Texas, on July 4, 1883. At the rodeo cowboys brave fierce bulls and wild broncos in a daring contest of riding and roping skills.

Texas Fortress

The Alamo in San Antonio, Texas, is called the "Cradle of Texas Liberty". It was used as a fortress in the Texas Revolution of 1836, when Texas won independence from Mexico.

State fact file

Iowa

2,926,324

Wild rose

 Eastern goldfinch

 Oak

Capital City: Des Moines

Nickname: Hawkeye State

Kansas

 2,688,418

 Native sunflower

 Western meadowlark

 Cottonwood

Capital City: Topeka

Nickname: Sunflower State

Missouri

 5,595,211

 Hawthorn

 Bluebird

 Dogwood

Capital City: Jefferson City

Nickname: Ozark State; Show Me State

The Great Plains States

The Great Plains are known as "America's breadbasket" because so much grain is grown there. North Dakota and Kansas produce more wheat than any other state, and Iowa grows the most corn.

American Buffaloes

The bison, or American buffalo, provided food, clothing, and shelter for the Native Americans of the Plains, and later for the white settlers. So many bison were hunted that they almost disappeared, but today they are protected.

Iowa is the only state bordered by two rivers – the Mississippi to the east and the Missouri to the west.

Mount Rushmore

The gigantic faces of four US presidents – Washington, Jefferson, Lincoln, and Theodore Roosevelt – are carved into Mount Rushmore in South Dakota. Gutzon Borglum started the carving in 1927, and his son finished it in 1941.

Did you know?

The ice-cream cone was invented in Missouri, at the St. Louis World's Fair in 1904.

Prairie Schooners

In the early 19th century, pioneers traveling across the Great Plains, to find new land to settle on, rode in covered wagons. They were nicknamed "prairie schooners" because they looked like sailing ships.

State fact file

Nebraska

 1,711,263

 Goldenrod

 Western meadowlark

 Cottonwood

Capital City: Lincoln

Nickname: Cornhusker State; Tree Planter State

North Dakota

 642,200

 Wild prairie rose

Western meadowlark

 American elm

Capital City: Bismarck

Nickname: Flickertail State; Peace Garden State

South Dakota

 754,844

 Pasqueflower

 Ring-necked pheasant

  Black Hills spruce

Capital City: Pierre

Nickname: Coyote State; Mount Rushmore State

State fact file

Illinois

 12,419,293

 Native violet

 Cardinal

 White oak

Capital City: Springfield

Nickname: Prairie State

Indiana

 6,080,485

 Peony

 Cardinal

 Tulip poplar

Capital City: Indianapolis

Nickname: Hoosier State

Michigan

 9,938,444

 Apple blossom

 Robin

 White pine

Capital City: Lansing

Nickname: Great Lake State; Wolverine State

The Great Lakes States

Ohio, Indiana, Illinois, Michigan, Wisconsin, and Minnesota all border the Great Lakes. Altogether, Michigan has more than 11,000 inland lakes and Minnesota has more than 15,000! Lake Superior is the largest freshwater lake in the world.

Detroit, Michigan, is famous for manufacturing cars and is nicknamed the "Motor City".

Great Lakes

The five Great Lakes – Michigan, Superior, Huron, Erie, and Ontario – make up Earth's largest area of fresh water. They are so large, that they can be seen from the moon, with the naked eye.

America's Dairyland

Wisconsin is sometimes called America's Dairyland. More milk and cheese is produced here than in any other US state. Fans of Wisconsin's *Green Bay Packers* football team even proudly call themselves "cheese heads"!

Tallest Building

The Sears Tower, in Chicago, Illinois, at 1,450 feet (442 m) is the tallest building in the USA. Luckily there is an elevator to get you to the top in 60 seconds!

Hot Dogs

The first hot dog ever, was served in Ohio, by Harry M. Stevens, in 1900.

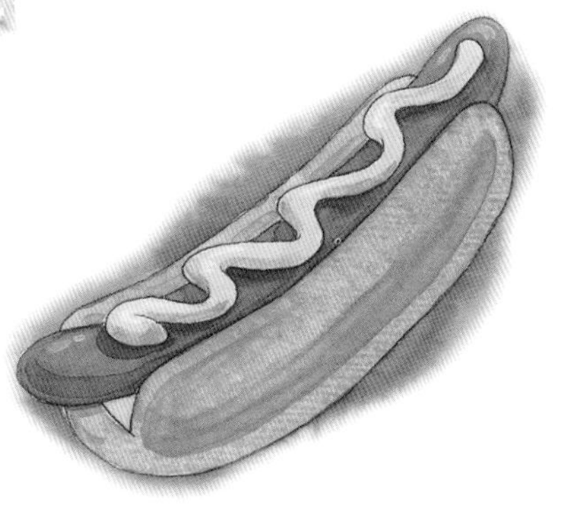

State fact file

Minnesota

 4,919,479

Lady's slipper

 Common loon

 Red pine

Capital City: St. Paul

Nickname: Gopher State; North Star State

Ohio

 11,353,140

 Scarlet carnation

 Cardinal

 Buckeye

Capital City: Columbus

Nickname: Buckeye State

Wisconsin

 5,363,675

 Wood violet

 Robin

 Sugar maple

Capital City: Madison

Nickname: Badger State

State fact file

Colorado

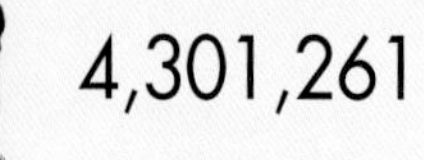
4,301,261

Rocky Mountain columbine

Lark bunting

Colorado blue spruce

Capital City: Denver

Nickname: Centennial State

Idaho

1,293,953

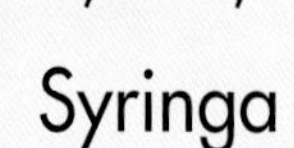
Syringa

Mountain bluebird

White pine

Capital City: Boise

Nickname: Gem State

Did you know?
Wyoming was the first state to give women the right to vote in 1869.

Rocky Mountain States

The Rocky Mountains form the backbone of Colorado, Wyoming, Idaho, and Montana. Some of America's most beautiful national parks are found here, including the very first one, Yellowstone in Wyoming.

Boiling Geysers

Old Faithful Geyser, in Yellowstone National Park, shoots about 8,400 gallons (38,186 liters) of boiling water 150 feet (46 m.) into the air, every seventy-six minutes. It has followed the same pattern for many years and that is why it is called "Old Faithful"!

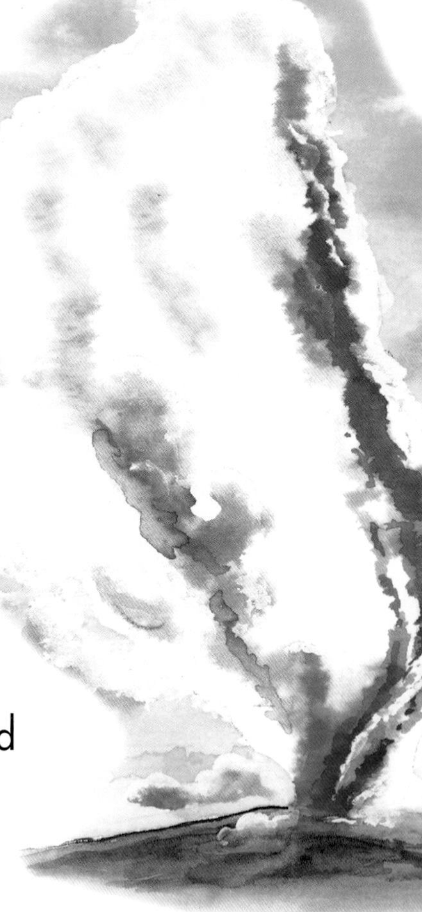

Mountain Wildlife

The Rocky Mountain states are famous for their wildlife. In fact, Montana has more elk, deer, and antelope than people!

Mile-High City

Colorado is America's highest state. Its capital, Denver, is called the "Mile-High City". *The Colorado Rockies* baseball team play at Coors Field. Most of the seats in the stadium are green, but if you sit in the row of purple seats you will be exactly one mile (1.6 km.) above sea level.

State fact file

Montana

 902,195

 Bitterroot

 Western meadowlark

 Ponderosa pine

Capital City: Helena

Nickname: Treasure State

Wyoming

 493,782

 Indian paintbrush

 Western Meadowlark

Cottonwood

Capital City: Cheyenne

Nickname: Equality State

Two-thirds of the potatoes grown in the USA come from Idaho.

State fact file

Arizona

 5,130,632

 Saguaro cactus blossom

 Cactus wren

 Paloverde

Capital City: Phoenix

Nickname: Grand Canyon State

Nevada

 1,998,257

 Sagebrush

 Mountain bluebird

 Single-leaf piñon; bristlecone pine

Capital City: Carson City

Nickname: Battle-born State; Sagebrush State; Silver State

Utah

 2,233,169

 Sego lily

 Seagull

 Blue spruce

Capital City: Salt Lake City

Nickname: Beehive State

Desert States

The desert states of Arizona, Utah, and Nevada are very dry. Nevada gets less rain than any other American state and also has more mountain ranges.

Nevada's Hoover Dam contains enough concrete to pave a two-lane highway from San Francisco to New York – that's almost 3,000 miles (4,828 km.)!

Grand Canyon

Arizona's Grand Canyon is the world's largest land gorge – 277 miles (446 km.) long and up to 18 miles (29 km.) wide at the rim. It gets five million visitors every year

Las Vegas

The casinos and nightclubs of Las Vegas in Nevada attract so many tourists that the city has more hotel rooms than any other place on Earth!

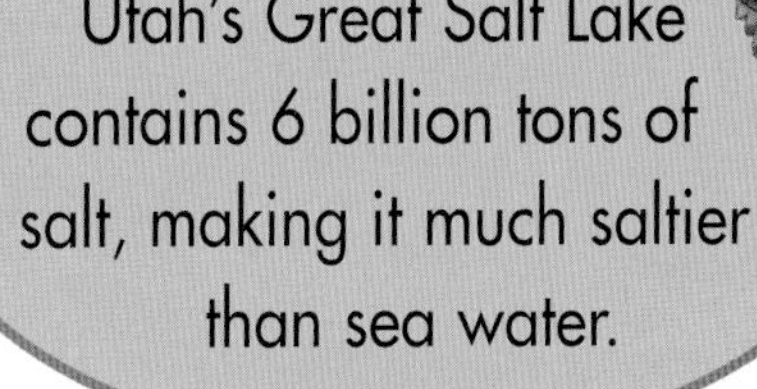

London Bridge

In 1962 the original London Bridge was sinking into the River Thames in London, England. The bridge was bought from the British government for $2,460,000 and shipped 10,000 miles (16,000 km.) to the USA in thousands of pieces. Block by block the bridge was rebuilt in Lake Havasu City, Arizona, and was finally completed in 1971.

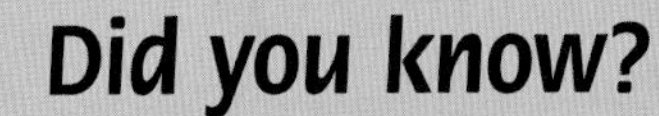

Did you know?

The Native American Havasupai tribe have lived in Havasu Canyon, part of the Grand Canyon, for more than 1,000 years.

State fact file

California

 33,871,648

 Golden poppy

 California valley quail

 California redwood

Capital City: Sacramento

Nickname: Golden State

Oregon

 3,421,399

 Oregon grape

 Western meadowlark

 Douglas fir

Capital City: Salem

Nickname: Beaver State

Washington

 5,894,121

 Western rhododendron

 Willow goldfinch

 Western hemlock

Capital City: Olympia

Nickname: Evergreen State

Pacific Coast States

California, Oregon, and Washington all share a coastline on the Pacific Ocean. California is one of America's busiest places. It has more people, cars, schools, and businesses than any other US state.

The Movies

Hollywood, in Los Angeles, California, is the world capital of the movie industry. The first film made here in 1908 was *The Count of Monte Cristo.*

The Boeing factory in Everett, Washington, where jumbo jets are assembled, is the world's largest building! It measures 472 million cubic feet (13.3 million cubic meters).

Tree Country

The Pacific coast is tree country! Possibly Earth's oldest living things are the bristlecone pines in California's Inyo National Forest, at about 4,700 years old, while the world's biggest tree is the Mendocino Tree in Ukiah, California – it is 367.5 feet (112 m.) tall and 44 feet (13 m.) around. Oregon also produces more timber than any other American state.

Did you know?

In 1848 gold was discovered near Sacramento, California. By 1849, thousands of people, known as "49ers", had come to join the "gold rush".

Disneyland

Disneyland, the first Disney theme park, was opened in Anaheim, California, in July 1955, with just 18 rides. Today there are over 60 attractions and Disneyland welcomes between ten and twelve million visitors every year.

State fact file

Alaska

 626,932

 Forget-me-not

 Willow ptarmigan

 Sitka spruce

Capital City: Juneau

Nickname: The Last Frontier

Alaska

Alaska became the 49th state on January 3, 1959. It is the coldest and the biggest state – 488 times bigger than Rhode Island.

Dog Mushing

Dog sleds were once the main form of transportation in Alaska. Today, "dog mushing", or dog-sled racing, is the official state sport.

Did you know?

America's biggest earthquake occurred in Alaska in March 1964.

Caribou

Alaska has almost twice as many caribou as people. Caribou are related to reindeer, and both males and females have antlers.

Alaska is the only American state to have coastlines on three different seas – the Arctic Ocean, the Pacific Ocean, and the Bering Sea.

Hawaii

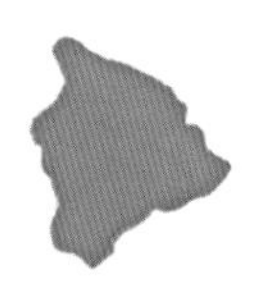

Hawaii became the 50th state on August 21, 1959. Hawaii has 122 tropical islands, with 8 main ones – Niihau, Kauai, Oahu, Molokai, Maui, Lanai, Kahoolawe (not inhabited), and Hawaii.

State fact file

Hawaii

 1,211,537

 Yellow hibiscus

 Hawaiian goose

 Kukui

Capital City: Honolulu

Nickname: Aloha State

Did you know?

Hawaii once had a king and queen, and ill has the only oyal palace in e USA – Iolani Palace, on the island of Oahu.

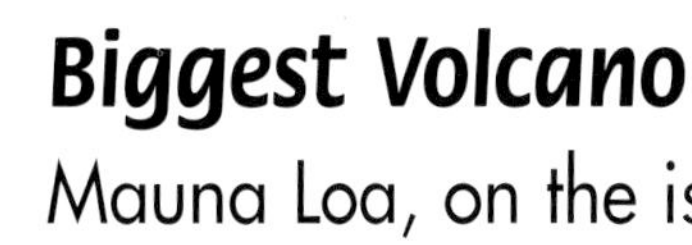

Biggest Volcano

Mauna Loa, on the island of Hawaii, is the biggest active volcano on Earth – it rises 3 miles (5 km.) from the bottom of the sea, and a further 2.6 miles (4.2 km.) above sea level.

Hawaiian Alphabet

The Hawaiian language has an alphabet of only 12 letters: A, E, H, I, K, L, M, N, O, P, U, and W.

Hawaii supplies more than one-third of all the world's pineapples.

ARKANSAS
CALIFORNIA REPUBLIC
DECEMBER 7, 1787
ILLINOIS
COMMONWEALTH OF KENTUCKY
IOWA
KANSAS
MONTANA
N C
OKLAHOMA
STATE OF OREGON
1859
THE SEAL OF THE STATE OF WASHINGTON
1889
WISCONSIN
1848